Catch 'em and Cook 'em

BUNNY DAY

Catch 'em and Cook 'em

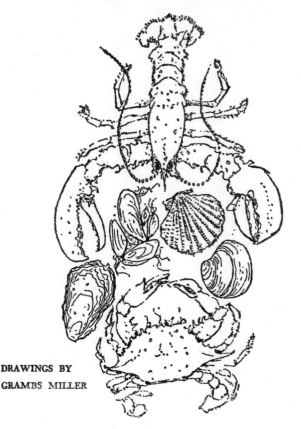

DRAWINGS BY
GRAMBS MILLER

GRAMERCY PUBLISHING COMPANY • NEW YORK

For my men HAROLD, PETER, JOEL

Contents

CONTENTS

Catch'em and Cook'em

YOU CAN DO IT TOO!

Some years ago I wrote a series of articles called "Catch 'Em and Cook 'Em" which ran in *Motor Boating* magazine. We had a small cabin cruiser then, *Day Dream*, and so many people threw seafood at me and said, "Frankly, I don't know what to do with it," that I felt sorry for them and tried to put down in writing for them simple and delicious ways to prepare the seafood.

Day Dream has gone long ago and in its place we have a little cottage on an inner creek that flows into the Peconic Bay on eastern Long Island. Every local treasure in the form of shellfish abounds in my little creek, and almost every day I can be found gathering it.

At the edge of the water, right in front of our cottage, at low tide we dig steamers.

Two yards out in the mud, and sometimes in a little sandbar, quahogs and cherrystones wait to be taken.

In a good year scallops play on the eel grass.

Across the creek, on the edge of the marsh, dwell oysters and mussels.

So in my little pram dinghy, which my son built, I am kept busy in front of my little cottage all summer long, catching the world's most delectable shellfish and then later cooking it inside the cottage.

And still many people come to me and say, "How do you

open those?" and "What do you do with them?" So what interests me now is to share the delight of the shellfish that are so plentiful in front of my cottage.

Oysters are oysters, clams are clams, crabs are crabs, all over the eastern seaboard. But after a recent trip to California, I find there is not too much difference in their shellfish. Many of my methods of catching and cooking shellfish at Towd Point could be deliciously used in San Francisco!

In what follows I have tried to show you not only how to obtain the shellfish, but how to open them, which is the main problem people have after they catch them.

There are many, many recipes about shellfish which you, no doubt, have on your shelves, so I have not tried to list all of them.

Instead I've written simple, easy-to-prepare, delightful recipes that *you* can cook in your own little summer camp or cottage anywhere that shellfish are to be found.

MAKE THE MOST OF GADGETS

To prepare these simple recipes, all you really need is a knife to open the shellfish and a pot to cook them in. But the stores are full of wonderful gadgets to make things easier for you, and to enhance the cooking and serving. So I had some fun browsing around in stores and this is what I came up with.

Clam knife
Clam ram
Scallop knife
Oyster shucker
Oyster knife
Food grinder
Clam steamer (10-quart!)
Shells for baking—Natural clam, crab, and abalone shells that have been dried and cleaned.

Or pottery shells, which are artificial scallop, crab, or clamshells and various-sized casseroles or ramekins.

Outdoor grill
Skewers
Lobster shears (same as poultry)
Lobster crackers
Lobster picks
Tongs

Butter melters
Paper bibs
Decorated platters
Seafood servers
Trivet

COLLECT SPECIAL EQUIPMENT

All you need to gather clams, crabs, oysters, etc. is a strong back, a pail, and a crab net. However, it is fun to add to your equipment and it will increase your take. So here is a list. Good hunting!

Pail
Crab net
Crab trap
Work gloves
Sneakers
Carpenter's apron (to tie around your middle so you can put the clams in the "nail pockets")
Clam fork
Clam rake
Old tire (to float basket or pail)
Lines
Wire
Wire basket (a friend made me a 2'×3' wire basket of close mesh which I staked in front of the cottage in the shallow water. In this I keep clams and oysters fresh.)
Scallop net
Wooden milk box
Flashlight

Clams

DO YOU KNOW YOUR CLAMS?

Littleneck

This is the hard or round clam when young and small. The size is suitable for eating raw on the half shell. Should be at least an inch and a half across.

Cherrystone

The hard clam when larger than the littleneck; about two inches in diameter.

Quahog

This is the large hard-shell or round clam, at least three inches in diameter. To be used in chowder, stuffed clams, etc.

Steamer

This is the soft or long clam, meaning that the shell is soft and that the clam is elongated, with a black neck. Also called longneck.

DIGGING STEAMERS

At the edge of the water at low tide steamer clams dwell. They reveal themselves to the hunter by tiny holes. If you throw a stone at these holes, the clams will squirt their juice. Immediately fall on your knees and dig with your hands the way a dog uses his paws. Steamers are deep burrowers, so persevere and you will be rewarded by the most delicate-flavored clams of all.

A few years ago there was a wonderful steamer bed right in front of my cottage, and they were just barely under the sand.

Then the next year I could find none. However, that was my fault. I discovered the little round holes and only dug a few inches down, to be disappointed.

What I found out was they had gone down really deep, and I had to go in up to my elbow to bring forth the largest, sweetest, meltiest, tenderest clams going. As with anything else, you have to work for something good.

We make a meal of these, steamed with melted butter, and fresh corn on the cob.

COOKING STEAMERS

STEAMED CLAMS

Wash fresh steamers. Put in saucepan with ½ cup of water. Cover tightly. Steam until all are open. Pour broth in cup; add a chunk of butter and pepper. Dunk clams into melted butter to your heart's desire.

STEAMER CHOWDER

24 steamer clams
½ onion, chopped
3 tablespoons butter
1 quart milk
¼ teaspoon salt
Dash pepper

Steam clams according to directions in preceding recipe, reserving juice. Yellow onion in the butter. Chop clams and add to onion with juice, milk, salt, and pepper. Heat just under the boiling point.

Serves 4.

DIGGING HARD CLAMS

I wish I could tell you just where to find clams, but I can't because they move, tides cover them, dredges destroy them, and clammers get too greedy. But at low tide, search harbors, bays, creeks, and inlets.

I prefer the toe method of getting them. Arm yourself with an old pair of gloves and wear sneakers on your feet. Choose a likely spot and feel around with your toe. If it strikes something hard, investigate with your hands. You might just happen on a bed of clams, as the hard-shells most of the time lie just under the surface of the mud or sand.

This year I learned a new method of digging hard-shell clams, and it can be very effective.

First, tie around your waist a line to which is attached an old-fashioned wooden milk box. Then wade, swim, or row to a nice muddy, weedy clam bed. (This new method came about because the nice sandy beds are being clammed out.)

Get on your hands, knees, and tummy and feel for those elusive hard-shells. This method brings good results, but unless the tide is awfully low, I almost drown, as I'm only 4'11". Besides, I have a horror of mud!

And many people get wonderful results with a rake, and the newest, most modern method is to use diving goggles.

But whatever way you dig them, it will be worth it because there is nothing more soul-satisfying than a really fresh clam.

HOW TO OPEN HARD CLAMS

When you try to open a littleneck or cherrystone clam, you will understand the expression "clam up." If you bruise a little fellow, you might as well put him away for a while; he'll resist you.

First, have the clams cold. This helps to lower their resistance.

Place the clam in the palm of your left hand, the short, fat end nearest your thumb. Place a small knifeblade between the two shells and press with the fingers of the same hand. Then wiggle the knife so the point can cut the muscle, which is down toward the hinge. The clam will loosen. Do the same thing to the top. Then take off the top shell and, with the knife, make sure you've separated all the muscles so you can slurp down the clam.

Some of my clam-digging friends put their haul in a freezer for a while. They claim this helps to open them.

I also have a very non-professional method if I want to eat tight ones immediately. I run them under very hot wa-

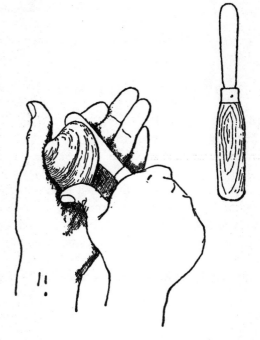

ter for a few seconds. I'm secretly ashamed of this "trick," but I really can't open them a mile a minute the way my son, Joel, does. I wish I could!

Quahogs may be opened the same way or by steaming.

JEAN'S CLAM APPETIZERS

2 dozen littleneck clams
1 cup dry, seasoned bread stuffing
8 slices of bacon, cut in thirds

Steam open clams. Grind them in a food chopper. Add the clams and their juice to the bread stuffing. If mixture is too runny, add more stuffing. Put the mixture back into the clamshell. Add a sliver of bacon on top and broil until bacon is crisp.

These are wonderful with drinks. Serves 4.

BEN'S CLAM APPETIZERS

Open ½ dozen cherrystones per person.
To each clam add:
A few drops of olive oil
A squeeze of lemon
A dash of black pepper
A sprig of chopped parsley
A dash of garlic salt

Place in a very hot oven or under the broiler and cook until clams are done—about 8 minutes.

CLAMS ON THE HALF SHELL

Littleneck or Cherrystone

½ dozen clams per person
Lemon wedges
Cocktail sauce

Wash and open clams. Serve chilled or on cracked ice with lemon wedges and cocktail sauce.

CLAM JUICE COCKTAIL

1 cup clam juice
1 cup tomato juice
1 teaspoon Worcestershire sauce
2 teaspoons lemon juice

Combine ingredients and chill in the refrigerator until ready to serve.
Serves 4.

BAKED CLAMS

Scrub a mess of hard clams or cherrystones. Place on a grill over a fire of red coals. The clams will open up and cook in their own juice. These are very tasty dipped in melted butter and washed down with the broth from the shell. These can also be done by placing clams in a shallow pan and leaving in a hot (450°) oven until they steam in their juice.
Nice with cocktails.

CLAMS CASINO

8 cherrystone clams per person
½ cup melted butter or olive oil
3 crushed garlic buds
3 tablespoons chopped parsley
1 teaspoon lemon juice
8 half slices of bacon

Soak everything but the clams and bacon together for several hours, letting all the flavors blend well. Open clams either with opener or by steaming. Drain a bit of juice off. On each clam place ½ to 1 teaspoon of the mixture. Place a piece of bacon on top.

Bake in hot oven (450°) for about 10 minutes, or until bacon is crisp and clams plumped.

TOMATO CLAM CHOWDER

1 quart ground clams and juice
¼ pound salt pork, cubed
1 large minced onion
3 minced carrots
4 cubed potatoes
1 16-ounce can tomatoes
1 10½-ounce can condensed tomato soup
2 bay leaves

Fry salt pork and onion until golden. Add clams and juice. Add prepared carrots and potatoes. Last of all, add tomatoes and tomato soup and bay leaves. This procedure is quite different from the one used in making regular clam chowder —so is the smooth consistency and tomatoey flavor.

Serves 4–6.

NEW ENGLAND CLAM CHOWDER

2 dozen or more ground clams and their juice
¼ pound salt pork, diced
1 large onion, diced
4 large boiled potatoes, peeled and diced
1 quart milk
Salt, pepper, flour

Fry salt pork and onion until golden. Add potatoes, barely cover with water, and boil until tender.

Add all but ½ cup of milk. Add seasonings and bring to boiling point. Add clams and broth. Thicken with a little flour blended with the remaining ½ cup of milk. Heat and serve piping hot with pilot crackers and tossed salad. The chowder will improve upon standing.

Serves 4.

LAST-MINUTE NEW ENGLAND CLAM CHOWDER*

1 10½-ounce can minced clams with liquid
1 10½-ounce can frozen potato soup, thawed
1 10½-ounce can light cream
4 tablespoons butter
¼ teaspoon salt
⅛ teaspoon pepper
4 tablespoons chopped chives

Mix all ingredients except chives and heat in a saucepan. Simmer lightly until butter melts.

Serve hot with chopped chives on top.

Serves 4.

* Almost the same as Quick Chowder II.

NEW YORK CLAM CHOWDER

1 dozen large hard clams, chopped, and juice
¼ pound salt pork, chopped
1 onion, chopped
1 cup cubed potatoes
1 carrot, sliced
1 16-ounce can tomatoes
½ teaspoon salt
¼ teaspoon pepper
2 cups hot water
1 teaspoon thyme

Brown pork; add onion and, when yellow, add potatoes, carrots, can tomatoes and salt, pepper, and water. Boil until potatoes and carrots are done. Add clams, thyme, and juice. Simmer for 5 minutes.

Serves 6.

QUICK CHOWDER I

1 dozen or more clams and juice
1 10½-ounce can condensed vegetarian vegetable soup

Chop clams and add with broth to soup.
Heat to boiling point and simmer for a few minutes.
Serves 3–4.

QUICK CHOWDER II

1 7½-ounce can minced clams with juice
1 13-ounce can potato soup (vichyssoise)
1 cup milk
¼ teaspoon salt
⅛ teaspoon pepper
⅛ teaspoon paprika
1 tablespoon butter

Dump all together and simmer gently for a few minutes.
Serves 3–4.

CURRIED CLAMS SOUTHAMPTON

1 can minced clams or 1 cup fresh with juice
1 cup fine bread crumbs
1 teaspoon chopped parsley
1 teaspoon curry powder
Dash of Tabasco sauce
Dash of Worcestershire sauce
Dash of salt and pepper
2 tablespoons mayonnaise

Mix clams, juice, crumbs, parsley, and seasonings with 1
tablespoon of the mayonnaise. Stuff buttered shells with
mixture. Spread remaining mayonnaise on top of each shell
and bake at 425° until mayonnaise is brown and bubbly,
about 15–18 minutes.
Fills three *large* clamshells.

DEVILED CLAMS (REGGIE)

1 dozen clams, chopped and drained
1 beaten egg
1 cup bread crumbs
⅓ cup catsup
1 teaspoon horseradish
¼ teaspoon thyme
½ teaspoon margarine
1 teaspoon minced parsley
1 tablespoon minced onion
1 tablespoon minced celery
¼ teaspoon salt
⅛ teaspoon pepper

Combine all ingredients and mix well. If mixture seems too runny, add more crumbs. Fill shells. Top with buttered crumbs and bake until brown.

Serves 4.

MAMA GEORGIE'S CLAM FRITTERS

1½ dozen clams with juice
Milk
½ cup flour
¼ teaspoon salt
½ teaspoon baking powder
1 egg, beaten

Wash clams and steam open. Chop fine. Drain, reserving juice. Measure clam liquid; add milk to make ¼ cup. Add chopped clams to dry ingredients; add beaten egg and liquid. Drop by spoonfuls into well greased frying pan. Cook until brown on both sides.

Serves 4.

BEN'S CLAM PIE (NORTHPORT)

1 quart clams
3 medium onions
6 medium potatoes
¼ pound salt pork
1 teaspoon sage
1 teaspoon diced celery leaves

Chop clams; dice onions and potatoes. Cut salt pork into small cubes. Fry until crisp. Pour off most of the fat.

Boil clams, onions, and potatoes in quart of liquid (clam juice plus water) for about 20 minutes. Add pork cubes, sage, and celery leaves. Put in baking dish. Cover with crust.

Bake 20 minutes in hot oven.

Serves 4.

RICH CRUST

2 cups flour
2 tablespoons shortening
Enough water to hold it
Pinch of salt

Toss lightly with a fork, then knead a few times on a lightly floured b   rd. Roll out ¼ inch thick.

ITALIAN CLAMS

1 dozen quahog clams, chopped
½ cup clam juice
1 cup bread crumbs
1 crushed garlic clove
¼ teaspoon salt
⅛ teaspoon pepper
1 teaspoon oregano
½ teaspoon basil
½ cup grated Parmesan cheese

Mix everything together except the cheese. Stuff back into the shells and sprinkle the top with cheese. Cook under the broiler until cheese is light brown.

Serves 4.

TOWD POINT CLAM PIE

1 dozen large quahogs and juice
1 large onion
3 tablespoons butter
2 tablespoons flour
1 cup milk
¼ teaspoon salt
⅛ teaspoon pepper
¼ teaspoon paprika

Chop onion and sauté it in butter until yellow; add flour and smooth. Add milk and clam juice and cook until thickened. Chop clams and add with seasonings. Put between unbaked pie crusts and bake in hot oven (450°) until crusts are brown, about 15 to 20 minutes.

Serves 4.

RED CLAM SPAGHETTI

2 cups chopped clams
2 tablespoons olive oil
2 crushed cloves garlic
1 medium onion, chopped
3 stalks celery, chopped
¼ teaspoon thyme
¼ teaspoon basil
¼ teaspoon oregano
¼ teaspoon Italian seasoning (optional)
½ teaspoon salt
⅛ teaspoon pepper
1 16-ounce can tomatoes
1 6-ounce can tomato paste
½ cup water
1 cup or more clam juice. Don't add water.
¼ cup chopped parsley
2 tablespoons butter

Heat oil in pan. Add garlic and onions and cook until transparent. Add celery and seasonings. Add tomatoes, tomato paste, water, clam juice, and parsley. Cook for one hour. Just before serving, add clams and butter.

Serve on spaghetti with Parmesan cheese on top.

Serves 4.

WHITE CLAM SPAGHETTI

1 7½-ounce can minced clams or 1 dozen chopped fresh
  clams and juice
3 tablespoons hot oil
1 diced onion
3 pressed buds of garlic
1 tablespoon flour
½ package of spaghetti

Heat oil (olive or salad) in bottom of pan. Sauté onion
and garlic in this till yellow. Add clams and juice. Smooth
a tablespoon of flour with water and thicken clam sauce.

Pour over enough cooked spaghetti for two.

BRIDGEPORT STUFFED CLAMS

Fresh large quahogs (about 3 per person)
1½ cup soft bread crumbs (if you have more clams, add
  more crumbs)
Salt and pepper to taste
Minced onion, green pepper, pickle, and chopped tomatoes
Bacon

Steam clams open. Remove top shell. Drain off clam broth.
You can prepare this in two ways; both are good.

Either you can chop your clams into your stuffing or leave
them whole and put the stuffing on top. I do it this way for
smaller, tender clams.

Make a mixture of the bread crumbs, salt, pepper, minced
onion, minced green pepper, chopped pickle, and chopped
tomatoes. Moisten this well with the clam liquid. It should
be quite moist and well seasoned.

Stuff clamshell full and put a half a piece of bacon on top of each. Bake in a hot oven (450°) until bacon is crisp and stuffing brown. Everyone will come back for more, and this is one of these dishes you can do in the winter with a can of minced clams.

PECONIC STUFFED CLAMS

15 large quahogs
2 cups seasoned bread stuffing
½ onion, minced
2 teaspoons minced parsley
½ cup chopped tomatoes
1 stalk celery
3 sweet gherkins, chopped
1 teaspoon Worcestershire sauce
2 tablespoons mayonnaise
Dash of Tabasco sauce
Salt and pepper to taste

Steam open and chop clams. Add with the juice to the rest of the ingredients and mix well. Stuff shells, top with bacon, and bake or broil until bacon is done.

Serves 5–6.

SHINNECOCK STUFFED CLAMS

1 dozen quahogs
1½ cups crumbled cheese crackers
¼ cup clam juice
1 tablespoon melted butter
½ minced onion
1 dash Tabasco sauce
1 teaspoon Worcestershire sauce
Salt and pepper to taste

Steam open and chop clams; mix with the cheese crackers. Moisten with their juice and the melted butter. Add the minced onion, Tabasco, Worcestershire sauce, and salt and pepper.

Stuff the mixture back into the shells. Top each with ½ slice of bacon and broil until crisp. Serves 4.

CLAM AND ZUCCHINI SQUASH CASSEROLE

2 dozen littlenecks
2 cups sliced squash
1 8-ounce can spaghetti sauce
Salt and pepper
1 cup bread crumbs
3 tablespoons melted butter

Cook squash (carefully, so it retains its shape) for 8 minutes. Steam open clams.

Place a layer of squash in buttered casserole. Add half the clams and their juice. Repeat. Add spaghetti sauce and seasonings. Mix crumbs and melted butter and top with these.

Bake at 450° for 20 minutes. Serves 4.

Crabs

CRABBING FUN

From late July on, the big "blue claws" run. By the hundreds they pour through the inlets, down the bays, under the bridges and pilings. They are as much fun to catch as to eat.

The equipment is simple—a piece of string, an old fish head or meat, and a crab net. Tie the fish head securely on the string and let it down in a spot where they're running. You'll know where the spot is because you can see them—and other crabbers will be there.

When the crab gets a good hold, pull him gently near the surface; then quickly scoop the net under him. Dump him from the net into your basket. Or if you have to pick him up, do so from the back so that those vicious claws don't get you.

THE CRAB TRAP

Several summers ago I invested in a crab trap. This is a wire contraption with four sides. A piece of cord is attached to each side, and each piece in turn is fastened to a long line in the center. So when the trap is pulled up by the line, the four sides close; when it is lowered to the bottom, the sides open and, of course, the crabs are supposed to stray in, being attracted, naturally, by bait.

So late one lovely afternoon a gang of us headed for Mecox Bay, one of our favorite crabbing spots.

With pieces of string I attached some lovely, old, ripe fish heads to the bottom of the trap and lowered it till it rested on the sand. I counted to sixty, then pulled it up as fast as I could. Two beautiful big, blue-claw crabs were clinging to the fish heads. They were dumped into a basket, and I followed the same procedure again. At the count of sixty I jerked it up and, if I remember correctly, I had three that time. Well, we were beside ourselves with glee and before long we had to stop because we had all we could eat.

I was tenderly folding up the trap when an old colored man, who had been sitting on a nearby bench watching me, ambled over and said:

"Lady, where did you get that thing? I'm going to get me one and go into the business."

That "thing" is also good to leave tied and lowered from a dock while you tend to other things. Check every once in a while and you may be well rewarded.

WHEN I WAS A LITTLE GIRL

Once a year, when I was a little girl in Maryland, my grandfather used to hire a launch and all the sisters, cousins, uncles, aunts, children, parents, and kin piled in and went down the Sinepuxent Bay for a day's fishing and fun. Many fish were caught. I remember I had a hand line once and a big one nearly pulled me out of the window, but for every fish there were more crabs caught than you could count.

So in the evening when we all arrived home, a big pot was put on the wood fire in the summer kitchen. Water, vinegar, and spices were brought to a boil. With much squealing and laughter, the live crabs were dumped in, not without one or two being spilled on the floor, which caused quite a commotion.

When the crabs were done, they were brought into the dining room, steaming, on huge platters. Cold glasses of beer soon appeared with pickles, cheese, and crackers, and everyone dove into the most wonderful feast ever. I was half asleep on someone's knee, but I can still taste those sweet crabs.

Nowadays, it would be a good idea to use a plastic cloth.

NIGHTTIME CRABBING

More recently, my boys I think will always remember one night several summers ago when someone said, "I'm hungry for crabs."

Before long, nets, string, baskets, fish heads, flashlights, and people piled into cars and headed for the Shinnecock canal. It was a beautiful summer night, but the most beautiful sight that greeted us was hundreds of large blue-claw crabs swimming next to the locks.

Night crabbing is great fun and different from daytime. If you shine a light on a crab, he will be attracted by it. Then, when you get his attention, you draw the light toward the bulkhead and he will follow it. Then all you have to do is to get the net under him and scoop him up.

That particular night the crabs were just itching to be

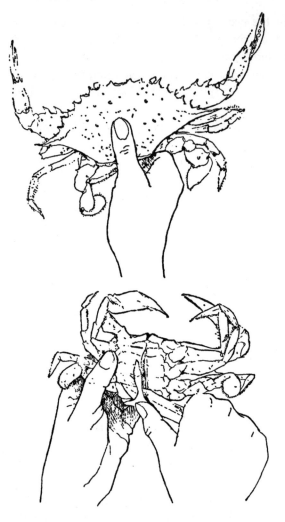

caught so, in no time at all, baskets were filled. However, in his eagerness to get an especially large one, my teen-age son, Joel, who was a good man with the net, fell in. Fortunately the crabs were afraid of him, and he got out unscathed.

Family, friends, and relations all went home, put a large pot on the gas stove with water, vinegar, and spices, and dumped the crabs in, not without spilling one or two.

We also had large glasses of cold beer, pickles, cheese, and crackers—and celebrated another memorable crab feast.

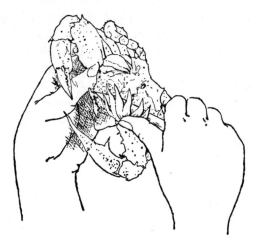

CLEANING CRABS

Cook and cool a live crab.

Turn it over so that the apron side is up. The apron is the underside, which has a design like an apron. With a sharp knife lift up the apron and tear it off. With knife, clean out lungs under the eyes. Peel off the "devil fingers"—the long, spongelike substance on each side under the topshell. Some people like to wash off the brown and green fat. Break the crab in half, crack the large claws, and you are ready for eating or picking out the meat for your favorite recipe.

SPICED CRABS (CRAB BOIL)

Bring a large pot of water to boil on a hot fire. Add about a half cup of vinegar and a teaspoon of salt and a teaspoon of a mixed spice called Shrimp or Crab Boil.

Throw in a mess of the largest blue-claw crabs you can catch. Cook at a fast boil from 5 to 10 minutes. Drain.

If you can't buy a package of Crab Boil, the nearest I can figure out is to throw in a pinch of whole cloves, several bay leaves, and a dash of allspice.

Pick the crabs hot; dunk in melted butter.

Or eat cold and dunk in chive mayonnaise.

Or just *eat*.

STEAMED CRABS

    1 dozen blue claws
    ½ cup vinegar
    Water
    3 bay leaves
    ¼ teaspoon whole cloves
    Pour the vinegar and water to a depth of one inch in a

large, heavy pot fitted with a trivet for steaming. Add the bay leaves and cloves and bring it to a boil. Dump the crabs into the trivet and steam for 10 minutes. Drain, cool, and clean them. Crack the claws; break the crabs in half and serve on a large platter. These with corn on the cob make a wonderful meal.

Serves 4–6.

STRONG COTTAGE
CRAB APPETIZERS

1 cup fresh crab meat
2 tablespoons mayonnaise
1 teaspoon curry powder
¼ teaspoon salt
⅛ teaspoon pepper
½ teaspoon Worcestershire sauce

Mix all ingredients together. Serve on crackers.

The gang next door served these and ate them with their cocktails while they watched the beautiful sunsets over Holmes' Hill.

Serves 4.

CRAB CAKE

2 cups flaked crab meat, fresh or canned
¼ teaspoon salt
⅛ teaspoon pepper
Dash Worcestershire sauce
1 egg, slightly beaten
Flour

Mix crab meat, salt, pepper, Worcestershire sauce, and egg. Shape into small cakes. Chill for several hours. When ready to cook, dredge with flour and fry in hot, deep fat for 2 to 3 minutes, or until light brown. Can also be sautéed in sweet butter. In deep fat, it's advisable to use a basket.

Serves 4.

DOTTIE'S CRAB CAKE

1 pound fresh crab meat (backfin, if possible)
2 tablespoons chopped parsley
1 teaspoon Worcestershire sauce
1 tablespoon mayonnaise
2 tablespoons (or less) cream
1 beaten egg
Salt and pepper to taste
Bread crumbs

Mix all ingredients except bread crumbs. Shape into cakes. Keep cold for several hours. Dredge in bread crumbs and sauté until brown.

Makes about 8 large cakes.

CRABS CREOLE

2 cups crab meat
1 large onion, chopped
1 crushed clove garlic
½ cup chopped green pepper
4 tablespoons bacon fat
1 16-ounce can tomatoes
½ cup chopped celery
1 teaspoon sugar
1 teaspoon Worcestershire sauce
Dash Tabasco sauce
½ teaspoon salt
⅛ teaspoon pepper

Sauté onion, garlic, and green pepper in bacon fat until tender. Add everything else and simmer for 20 minutes. Serve on rice. Serves 4.

CRAB BISQUE

- 1 6½-ounce can crab meat, or 1 cup fresh
- 1 10½-ounce can condensed tomato soup
- 1 10½-ounce can condensed green pea soup
- 1 10½-ounce can water
- 1 10½-ounce can milk
- ¼ teaspoon salt
- ⅛ teaspoon pepper

Combine everything and heat. Don't cook too long.
Serves 6.

DEVILED CRABS

- 1 cup crab meat (fresh or canned)
- 1 cup bread crumbs
- ½ cup minced celery
- 1 egg, slightly beaten
- ½ cup minced green pepper
- 1 teaspoon prepared mustard
- 1 tablespoon Worcestershire sauce
- ¼ teaspoon pepper
- ½ teaspoon salt
- Dash of Tabasco
- 2 tablespoons lemon juice
- ½ cup melted butter or margarine

Mix ingredients together well and stuff into crab shells or
individual baking dishes. Place in hot oven (375°) for about
12 to 15 minutes.
Serves 2–3.

CRAB MEAT AU GRATIN

1 6½-ounce can crab meat or 1 cup fresh crab meat
2 cups white sauce
1 cup grated sharp cheese
Salt and pepper to taste
1 teaspoon Worcestershire sauce

Mix white sauce and crab meat. Add cheese. Season with a touch of salt, pepper, and Worcestershire sauce.

Stuff buttered crab shells or individual baking dishes. Pop into 425° oven; bake until golden brown.

This is also delicious when you omit the cheese; add 2 tablespoons of sherry instead. Cover the top with buttered crumbs or mayonnaise and bake at 425° for 10 to 15 minutes.   Serves 4.

MARYLAND CRAB IMPERIAL

2 cups backfin crab meat
4 tablespoons melted butter
¼ onion, chopped
4 teaspoons chopped fresh parsley
1 tablespoon mayonnaise
2 tablespoons cream
1 teaspoon Worcestershire sauce
Salt and pepper to taste

Sauté onion in butter.

Mix all ingredients well. Pile into crab shells or individual baking dishes. Spread extra mayonnaise on top.

Bake at 350° for ½ hour.

Serves 4.

CRAB GUMBO (SOUTHERN)

2 dozen large blue crabs
1 medium onion, chopped
1 green pepper
1 tablespoon butter or bacon fat
1 tablespoon flour
1 16-ounce can tomatoes
Salt and pepper to taste
1 teaspoon sugar
1 15½-ounce can okra or 1 package frozen
¼ teaspoon celery salt
1 bay leaf

Boil crabs, drain, and clean. Break into halves or quarters. Fry onions and green peppers in fat until golden. Add flour and stir until brown. Add tomatoes, salt, pepper, sugar, okra, celery salt, and bay leaf. Heat crabs thoroughly in this mixture and serve with rice on the side.
Serves 6.

CRAB NEWBURG

1 6½-ounce can crab meat or 1 cup fresh
2 cups white sauce
3 tablespoons sherry
½ teaspoon salt
⅛ teaspoon pepper
1 teaspoon prepared mustard
1 teaspoon Worcestershire sauce

Mix all together and heat gently. Serve on toast points.
Serves 4.

CRAB RAVIGOTE

    1 6½-ounce can crab meat (or 1 cup fresh)
    ¼ teaspoon salt
    ⅛ teaspoon pepper
    ⅛ teaspoon cayenne pepper
    1 teaspoon prepared mustard
    1 tablespoon oil
    ½ tablespoon chopped parsley
    1 tablespoon chopped celery
    1 hard-cooked egg, chopped
    3 tablespoons vinegar

Season crab meat with salt, pepper, cayenne, and mustard. Add remaining ingredients. Put in crab shells; spread evenly with mayonnaise and serve very cold. Delicious!
    Serves 2.

CRAB SPECIAL

    1 6½-ounce can crab meat or 1 cup fresh
    1 tablespoon mayonnaise
    1 tablespoon green pepper, minced
    1 tablespoon red pepper, minced
    ¼ teaspoon salt
    ⅛ teaspoon pepper
    1 teaspoon Worcestershire sauce
    1 egg, slightly beaten

Mix everything together and stuff into shells. Spread extra mayonnaise on each. Bake at 425° for 10–15 minutes.
    Serves 3.

CRAB MEAT À LA RECTOR

1 cup crab meat
½ green pepper, diced
½ medium onion, diced
1 16-ounce can tomatoes
½ teaspoon Worcestershire sauce
¼ teaspoon salt
⅛ teaspoon pepper
1 teaspoon sugar
2 hard-cooked eggs, sliced
1 cup bread crumbs
2 tablespoons butter

Mix the green pepper, onion, tomatoes, crab meat, seasonings, and sugar together. Spread mixture in a buttered casserole. Layer sliced eggs next. Top with crumbs and dot with butter. Bake at 300° for one hour.
Serves 4.

CRAB MEAT AND SMITHFIELD HAM

1 cup crab meat
2 medium slices Smithfield ham or smoked ham
2 tablespoons butter

Sauté the ham in the butter. Put aside and keep warm while you sauté the crab meat in the same pan for about 3 minutes. Serve the crab meat on the ham.
Serves 2.

STUFFED CRABS

4 large crabs
1 cup bread crumbs
6 tablespoons butter, melted
½ onion, chopped
1 teaspoon parsley
¼ teaspoon salt
⅛ teaspoon pepper
¼ teaspoon sage
¼ teaspoon thyme
2 teaspoons mayonnaise
¼ teaspoon paprika

Boil and clean crabs.

Mix the bread crumbs, melted butter, onion, and seasonings together. Stuff the cavities of the crabs with this mixture. Spread them evenly with mayonnaise and sprinkle the paprika on top. Bake at 350° for 25 minutes.

Serves 4.

CRAB SOUP

2 short ribs of beef
2 quarts water
1 tablespoon salt
2 carrots, diced
½ small head of cabbage, chopped
1 large onion, chopped
½ bunch celery, diced
½ bunch parsley, chopped

6 boiled blue-claw crabs
½ package frozen corn
½ package frozen lima beans
½ package frozen peas
¼ cup barley

Cook the first eight ingredients for one hour. Add the rest of the ingredients and cook for ½ hour. Before serving, remove crab aprons and clean the crabs, break them in half, remove the meat from the claws, and add to soup.

Serves 12.

CRAB MEAT WITH WALNUTS

2 cups picked crab meat
½ cup chopped walnuts
1 hard-cooked egg, chopped
2 tablespoons parsley
½ teaspoon salt
⅛ teaspoon pepper
1 teaspoon Worcestershire sauce
½ teaspoon prepared mustard
Dash Tabasco sauce
¾ cup mayonnaise

Mix all ingredients together except ¼ cup mayonnaise. Spoon into crab shells or baking shells. Spread remaining mayonnaise on top of each. Bake at 400° for 25 minutes.

Fills 4–6 shells.

CRAB MEAT AND SHRIMP

8 extra-large jumbo shrimp, cleaned
1 cup crab meat
1 tablespoon mayonnaise
1 teaspoon chopped parsley
½ teaspoon salt
⅛ teaspoon pepper
1 egg
1 tablespoon water
1 cup fine bread crumbs

Cut three quarters of the way through the shrimp. Mix the crab meat with the mayonnaise, parsley, salt, and pepper and fill the shrimp cavities with this mixture. Beat egg with water and dip each filled shrimp into the mixture. Roll in bread crumbs. Fry in a basket in deep fat for 3 to 4 minutes. Ambrosia!

Serves 3–4.

SOFT-SHELL CRABS

A soft-shell crab is one which is molting, or shedding its hard shell. They are usually available only from June until September and not terribly plentiful at that, as you have to catch the crab at just the exact moment he's undressed. They are considered a great delicacy.

"Softies" are usually quite lethargic, and you can pick them up from the bottom on a day when the water is clear—or one might happen to stroll into your trap if you're real lucky.

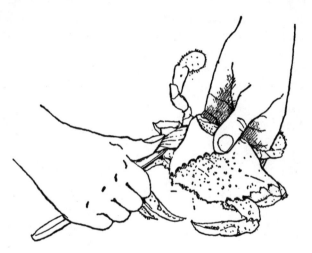

CLEANING SOFT-SHELL CRABS

You can handle a live soft-shell crab because it's not its usual scrappy self. Remove the apron and clean out the lung-like substance under the eyes. Then with a sharp knife probe under the top shell and scrape out the "devil fingers," the long, spongy stuff. You're all set then.

COOKING SOFT-SHELL CRABS

BROILED SOFT-SHELL CRABS

4 large soft-shell crabs
4 tablespoons butter
4 teaspoons lemon juice

Lay crabs in broiler pan. Put a tablespoon of butter on each. Sprinkle a teaspoon of lemon juice on each one. Broil for 5 minutes. Turn, ladle some of the pan butter and lemon juice on each, and broil for 5 minutes more.

Serves 4.

FRIED SOFT-SHELL CRABS

Use 2 small soft-shell crabs per person.
1 egg, slightly beaten
¼ cup water
½ cup flour or ½ cup cracker crumbs
Fat for frying

Mix egg and water. Dip the crabs in this mixture then roll in the flour or cracker crumbs. Have hot fat a half inch deep in a skillet. Fry for 10 minutes.

Serve on toast with lemon wedges and tartare sauce.

SAUTÉED SOFT-SHELL CRABS

1 large soft-shell crab or 2 small ones per person
½ cup butter

Melt the butter in a skillet. Sauté the crab for 5 minutes.
Turn and sauté 5 minutes more, or until golden brown.
Serve on a slice of toast with a sliver of lemon and tartare
sauce on the side.

Lobsters

BUYING LOBSTERS

Someday there will be lobsters in my little creek, because several times I have seen tiny baby lobsters, but in the meantime I have to buy them.

My neighbors and I often have a jaunt to Montauk to pick out the fresh ones for a beach feast, but fortunately we can always buy wonderful ones right in town, and in June they are the fattest and least expensive.

And so it is all along the eastern seaboard: one can buy the best, freshest lobsters—except on the Maine coast, where I understand people have lobster pots instead of lawns!

I think the best eating lobsters weigh 1½ to 2 pounds. They are tender, sweet, and satisfying.

However, one day I sent my son, Joel, out to buy some for a party and, to my dismay, he came home with a 10-pound one. After much fussing we borrowed a new garbage pail and boiled him. He was delicious!

Make sure you purchase a live, wiggling lobster, and don't be afraid. The claws are usually pegged. Keep it in a cool place until ready to prepare.

CLEANING LOBSTERS

For lobster broil, place a *live* lobster on its back on a cutting board. With your left hand hold the head down and with your right plunge a sharp knife in the top of the dividing line and split all the way to the tail. With both hands crack open. Remove the intestines and the sac under the head.

If the red stuff is there, keep it in or use it in a stuffing. It's the roe, or coral, and it's very good. The green stuff is good also. It is called tomalley.

For steaming or boiling a lobster, hold it by the back of the head and plunge it into boiling water. Don't be squeamish; the result is worth the trouble.

After you steam or boil a lobster, clean it the same way as a live one.

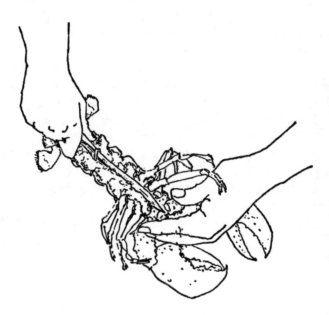

COOKING LOBSTERS

BOILED LOBSTERS

1- to 1½-pound lobster per person
Large kettle of boiling water.

Plunge lobster quickly into rapidly boiling water. Cover tightly and boil 20 minutes.

Remove and split and clean.

Serve hot with melted butter and lemon juice, or serve cold with mayonnaise.

BROILED LOBSTER

1- to 2-pound lobster per person
1½ cup stuffing per lobster (see lobster stuffings)
Melted butter
Lemon juice
Lemon wedges

If you are going to broil the lobsters soon after you purchase them, your fishman can split and clean them for you. Otherwise, split and clean your lobsters.

Fill the cavity with a stuffing of your choice and brush melted butter over the flesh. Sprinkle lemon juice over this.

Place on a broiler, flesh side to the flame, about 2 to 3 inches away. Cook for about 10 minutes, basting every 5 minutes with melted butter. Flesh should be nice and white when done, and tender when tested with a fork. When in doubt, allow a few more minutes.

Serve with melted butter and lemon wedges.

CHARCOAL-BROILED LOBSTER

1- to 2-pound lobster per person
Plenty of melted butter
½ cup lemon juice
Red-coal charcoal fire

Place split and cleaned lobsters shell side down on the grill over a hot fire. Brush the flesh with melted butter and sprinkle this with lemon juice. Broil for 10 minutes. Turn fast and broil shell side about 6 minutes. Turn up again and brush with melted butter. They should be done, but test with fork; flesh should separate easily. Serve with the rest of the melted butter and lemon juice.

We love to have this feast on the beach by the ocean.

We use paper plates for the lobster and paper cups for the melted butter and lemon juice.

The scent of the salt air, mingled with the charcoal smoke and lobster aroma, almost drives one crazy with hunger.

MAINE STEAMED LOBSTERS

1- to 1½-pound lobster per person
1 inch water in a large pan

Plunge lobsters in steaming water quickly to kill them.
Cover and steam 20 minutes.
Take out, clean, and serve with lemon juice and melted butter.

My husband was squeamish about this method. However, I learned it from a friend who spends all her summers in Maine and I must say the lobsters are always tender and delicious.

LOBSTER ROLLS

1 cup lobster meat
6 tablespoons butter
3 tablespoons sherry
¼ teaspoon salt
⅛ teaspoon pepper
1 teaspoon Worcestershire sauce
2 buttered and toasted hamburger rolls

Melt butter. Sauté lobster in it for a few minutes. Add sherry and seasonings and serve on hot, toasted rolls.
Serves 2.

VERA'S LOBSTER ROLLS

1 6½-ounce can or 1 cup chopped lobster meat
½ cup cubed Swiss cheese
2 tablespoons minced onion
¼ teaspoon salt
¼ cup mayonnaise
1 teaspoon vinegar
4 hamburger buns

Toss everything together. Spread hamburger buns with butter. Then spread with lobster mixture. Wrap each bun in foil. Bake at 350° for 20 minutes. Cool for 5 minutes before opening. Wonderful for lunch!
Serves 4.

JAN'S LOBSTER WITH CLAM JUICE

1 lobster per person
2 cups fresh or bottled clam juice

Heat clam juice in a large heavy kettle. Plunge lobsters in head down. Cover tightly.
Steam for 20 minutes.

LOBSTER SAUCE

1 cup lobster meat
2 cups medium cream sauce
½ teaspoon salt
⅛ teaspoon pepper
1 teaspoon Worcestershire sauce
2 tablespoons sherry

Add lobster, seasonings, and sherry to the cream sauce. Heat through.
Wonderful served on rolls.
Wonderful to dip toast points in at a cocktail party.
On rolls serves 4.
For cocktails serves 8.

LOBSTER STUFFINGS

CLAM STUFFING

1 cup bread crumbs
½ cup chopped clams
½ cup clam juice

Mix everything together and stuff back into shell. Enough for two 1- to 2-pound lobsters.

CORAL STUFFING

1 cup bread crumbs
4 tablespoons melted butter
Salt and pepper to taste
Coral (red) and tomalley (green stuff) from lobster

Mix everything together and stuff back into shell cavity. I think this is the best stuffing ever. Unfortunately, you don't always have the coral, which is the roe in a female lobster.

This amount stuffs 2 lobsters.

PLAIN STUFFING

1 cup bread crumbs
4 tablespoons melted butter
Salt and pepper to taste

Mix everything together and stuff into lobster cavity.

This amount should stuff about two 1- to 1½-pound lobsters.

CRAB MEAT STUFFING

1 cup bread crumbs
½ cup crab meat
4 tablespoons melted butter
Salt and pepper to taste
Dash Worcestershire sauce

Mix everything together and stuff into lobster shell.
Enough for two 1- to 2-pound lobsters.

Mussels

HOW TO GATHER AND PREPARE THEM

Across the creek from our little cottage grow the most abundant, most delectable, and most neglected mollusks—the mussels.

I can thank my brother for introducing me to these blue-black beauties many years ago aboard his boat.

Few people know about mussels, especially Americans. But speak to a Frenchman or a Belgian and he will go into ecstasies.

I have only a few recipes for mussels, compared to the number I have for clams, but each year I add one more recipe and I always think it is the best.

Blue-black mussels cling to rocks, wharves, and mud. It is best to pick them at low tide because the fresh, live ones would be exposed at that time. Mussels cling by means of a beard. So when you pull a mussel from its home, be sure there is some resistance and that some of the beard is still visible. The beard is a sign that the mussel is alive.

Dead mussels, which become filled with mud, abound. They are the same weight as live mussels and pressure on the shells with the thumb does not always open them. I call these fakes "mudders." Fortunately, if you get one in the pot by mistake, it will not open by itself and spill out the mud.

The only way to gather mussels is to pull them off by hand, and experience will soon show you the perfect ones.

They need stiff scrubbing with a wire brush, and you must pull off the beard.

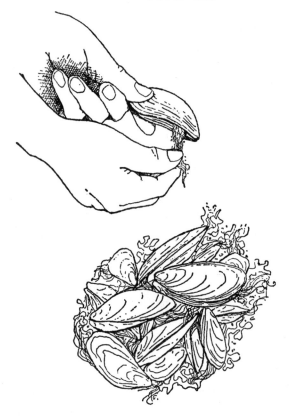

HOW TO OPEN MUSSELS

The only method I know to open mussels is to steam them. Put them in a large pot with ¼ cup of water. If by any chance one or several remain closed after steaming, do not investigate. Throw them away immediately, because they will contain mud (but fortunately these will not open and spill in the pan).

COOKING MUSSELS

STEAMED MUSSELS

Scrub and unbeard mussels.
Place in pot with ¼ cup of white wine, preferably Chablis.
Steam until open.
Serve with the broth and with melted butter on the side.
If these are the main dish, I suggest at least 1 dozen per person.

MUSSEL APPETIZER VINAIGRETTE

24 mussels
4 tablespoons vinegar
¼ teaspoon salt
⅛ teaspoon pepper
6 tablespoons olive oil
1 tablespoon chopped green pepper
1 tablespoon chopped pickle
1 tablespoon chopped parsley
1 teaspoon sugar
1 tablespoon chopped chives or scallions

Clean and steam open mussels and let cool.
Remove cooled mussels from the shells. Mix all other ingredients together and chill the mussels in the mixture in the refrigerator for several hours.
Serve very cold in a platter with a bowl of crackers on the side.
Serves 4.

MUSSELS IN BACON

24 mussels
¼ cup water
12 slices bacon
4 tablespoons parsley

Scrub and beard mussels. Steam open in a kettle with the water.

Remove from shell. Wrap a half slice of bacon around each mussel. Broil until bacon is done, turning once. Serve on buttered toast with a sprinkling of parsley on top.

Serves 4.

BELGIAN MUSSELS

4 dozen mussels
1 minced onion
1 minced garlic bud
1 tablespoon bacon fat
1 tablespoon butter
1 tablespoon olive oil
½ cup white wine
3 tablespoons chopped parsley

Cook onion and garlic in the bacon fat, butter, and olive oil until onions are yellow. Add mussels. Pour wine over mussels and add chopped parsley. Steam until mussels open wide—about 20 minutes.

Serves 3–4.

ROUX

2 egg yolks
2 tablespoons cream

Beat egg yolks and cream with a fork. Add 1 cup of broth from the steamed mussels. Stir until thick over low fire or double boiler, being careful not to overcook. Add more broth if needed. Serve mussels with top shell removed and the roux poured on top.

Serves 3–4.

FRENCH MUSSELS

1 dozen mussels per person
1 chopped shallot
¼ cup Chablis
Pinch thyme
⅛ teaspoon ground pepper
2 tablespoons chopped fresh parsley
2 tablespoons butter
1½ tablespoons flour

Scrub and unbeard mussels. Place in pot with wine, herbs, and seasoning, and steam until shells open. Then remove the top shells and place mussels on a large platter.

In another pan melt the butter and add the flour; make into a paste. Carefully add the stock from the mussels, stirring constantly until the sauce is the consistency of a thin gravy. Pour the sauce over the mussels.

Serve these with French bread so that you can sop up this wonderful juice.

ITALIAN MUSSELS

- 3 dozen mussels
- 3 tablespoons olive oil
- 1 teaspoon chopped hot red pepper
- 3 crushed garlic cloves
- 3 tablespoons chopped parsley
- ½ teaspoon oregano

Heat olive oil and sauté chopped peppers and garlic for a few minutes. Add mussels, chopped parsley, and oregano. A spot of red wine adds to the flavor and helps start the steaming. Cover and steam until opened.

This can be served hot or chilled.

Serves 3.

DAVIS CREEK STUFFED MUSSELS

- 2 dozen mussels
- 3 tablespoons butter
- ½ medium onion, minced fine
- 1 tablespoon chopped parsley
- ½ teaspoon sage
- ¼ teaspoon salt
- ⅛ teaspoon pepper
- 1½ cups bread crumbs

Clean and steam open the mussels. Remove the top shell. Sauté the onion in the butter until the onion is yellow. Dump in everything else and mix well. Spread the stuffing over each mussel in its half shell and put under the broiler for a few minutes, or until the top is light brown.

Serves 2–4.

MUSSELS MARINARA

Use at least 1 dozen mussels per person.
Scrub and unbeard mussels.
Place in pot and pour over them one 8-ounce can of
marinara sauce.
Steam until open.
Serve over spaghetti with Italian bread on the side.

MUSSELS À LA RUSSE

2 dozen mussels
1 cup mayonnaise
½ cup chili sauce

Clean and steam open the mussels. Cool and remove from
their shells. Mix the mayonnaise and chili sauce. Add the
mussels to this mixture and chill well. Serve on a bed of
lettuce as an appetizer or salad.
Serves 4.

Oysters

I will always be reminded of one bright, cold March day when, driving back to New York from Southampton, my neighbor and I stopped at the Shinnecock canal to buy some fresh flounders.

The fishman, who sells from an old boat there, tried to persuade me to buy some oysters.

To his amazement and that of a couple standing nearby, Elise Flanagan and I cried, "Oysters? Buy oysters? Why, we have a bushelful right in this car." And to prove it we held up several huge ones.

The eyes of the men nearly popped out, and they promptly wanted to know where we got them. "Oh," we said casually, "right in front of our cottage."

"Well," said one, "I'll tell you what I'll do. I'll come and help you dig them and I'll give you half."

"No thank you, sir. We don't even have to dig them. We just pick them up."

Which was true.

On that particular day we had driven to check a robbery in the cottage. Naturally we went out front to look at the water, and there was a phenomenally low tide—lower than we had ever seen—and flats undiscovered by us were exposed. Lying in the mud with the lips just barely showing were dozens of oysters.

We immediately pounced on them and took home a bushel of the most delicious oysters we ever ate.

It's never happened again, I might add.

GATHERING OYSTERS

At low tide one can see the succulent oysters clinging to the mudbanks in the marshes. Sometimes they are just above the water, sometimes just under. Float along in a rowboat and pull them from the banks. If the water is extra clear—and it is very often unusually clear in September, when it is permissible to gather them—the lips of the deep ones can be seen open for air. It is advisable to use gloves because the edges of the oysters are sometimes very sharp.

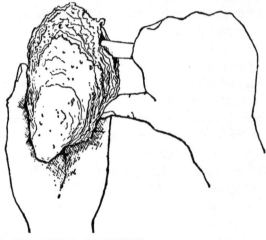

HOW TO OPEN OYSTERS

Place the oyster mound side down. If you look at one oyster sideways, you'll notice one side is fatter than the other; this I call the mound.

With a hammer or oyster opener hammer off the excess lip until you see a slight opening. Force tip of knife into opening and slide it up and under till you can slice the muscle. Do the same on the upper side. Take off upper shell and there you leave the oyster ready for anything—especially eating!

COOKING OYSTERS

OYSTERS ON THE HALF SHELL

Oysters—½ dozen per person
Ice
Cocktail sauce

Wash oysters and chill thoroughly. Open and serve on cracked ice with cocktail sauce and saltines.

ROASTED OYSTERS

Oysters in shell—½ dozen per person
Wash oysters thoroughly and chip shells.
Place in oven pan and cook in 450° oven until open. It takes about 20 minutes.
Remove top shell and serve in the deep half.
Good with salt, pepper, and lemon juice.
Good with vinegar sauce.
Good with cocktail sauce.
Good with cocktails!

ROBINS ISLAND OYSTERS

1 pint cleaned oysters and juice
2 tablespoons butter
½ cup medium cream
¼ teaspoon nutmeg
2 tablespoons sherry
¼ teaspoon salt
⅛ teaspoon pepper

Sauté oysters in the butter for a few minutes. Add cream, nutmeg, sherry, salt, and pepper. Warm through (do not boil) and serve on toast.

Serves 3–4.

SAUTÉED OYSTERS

1 dozen oysters
2 tablespoons butter
½ cup thin cream
1 teaspoon chopped parsley
¼ teaspoon salt
⅛ teaspoon pepper
Dash Tabasco sauce

Melt butter; add oysters and cook until edges curl. Then add cream, parsley, and seasonings and stir until warm. Serve on toast.

Serves 2.

SCAILOPED OYSTERS

- 1 pint oysters with their liquor
- 1 cup cracker crumbs
- ¼ teaspoon salt
- ⅛ teaspoon pepper
- ½ cup butter
- 1 cup medium cream
- ½ teaspoon nutmeg
- ½ teaspoon Worcestershire sauce
- 2 or 3 drops Tabasco sauce
- 1 cup bread crumbs

In a buttered casserole put a layer of cracker crumbs; cover with half the oysters. Sprinkle with salt and pepper, and dot with butter and half the cream, nutmeg, Worcestershire sauce and 1 drop of Tabasco. Cover with the bread crumbs and repeat the oyster mixture, adding the rest of the cream, liquor, and seasonings. Lastly, cover with the remaining crumbs, dot with butter, and bake 30 minutes at 400°.

Serves 4.

OYSTER STEW

- 1 pint oysters with their liquor
- 1 quart milk with top milk
- ¼ teaspoon salt
- ⅛ teaspoon pepper
- 4 tablespoons butter

Cook oysters in their liquor until the edges curl. Add milk, salt, pepper, and butter, and heat to just under boiling point or milk will curdle. Serve with large oyster crackers.

Serves 4.

OYSTERS IN WHITE WINE

1 pint oysters
1 cup white wine
¼ teaspoon salt
⅛ teaspoon pepper
1 onion, sliced
1 tablespoon parsley
1 bay leaf
½ teaspoon thyme

In a saucepan or chafing dish bring the white wine with seasonings and herbs to a simmer. Add the oysters and cook gently until the edges curl.

Serves 3.

STEAMED OYSTERS

Oysters in shell—½ dozen per person
½ cup water
½ teaspoon Worcestershire sauce
½ teaspoon lemon juice

Wash oysters.

Chip excess shell off the end of each oyster.

Place in kettle. Add water, Worcestershire sauce, and lemon juice. Put cover on tightly and steam until open. It takes about 15 minutes.

Remove top shells and serve on a platter with a sauce of your choice on the side. I recommend cocktail sauce, or hot butter sauce, or plain melted butter.

FRIED OYSTERS

1 pint oysters
1 egg
1 tablespoon water
1 cup fine bread crumbs
Salt and pepper to taste

Drain oysters and pat dry with a paper towel. Beat egg with water and add salt and pepper to taste. Dip each oyster into this mixture and roll in crumbs. Place the oysters in a wire basket and deep-fat-fry for 3 to 4 minutes. Or fry in shallow fat and turn once after 2 minutes.

Serve on a platter with tartare sauce, lemon wedges, chili sauce, and cole slaw. Serves 2–3.

I love the large Chincoteague oysters. However, they are not easily obtainable, so I put two oysters together and dip them into the egg mixture and bread crumbs *twice*. This holds them together.

Scallops

HOW TO GET THEM

On the sixteenth of September there is a change on the Peconic Bay, and in all the little harbors, inlets, and creeks that are in the area. For on that day it is legal to take those tiny, sweet, tender bay scallops for which the Peconic is famous.

Every man, woman, boy, and girl who can get out on the water is there. They pick up the scallops with nets of every shape and form; they pick them up with their hands, when the tide is low enough and when it is a plentiful year. They are easy to get because they lie on the mud, sand, or weeds. The gulls join the people in scalloping, and they know where to find the largest.

HOW TO OPEN SCALLOPS

Place the scallop in your left hand, dark side down. Insert the blade of a knife (you can buy a scallop knife if you wish) in the hinge. Scoop the knife 'way down in the fat area in the bottom. Cut the muscle; then do the same on the top. Open. Pull the little white muscle from the rest of the scallop. That is your pearl. After you do a pail of these, you will not be greedy—because a half a bushel yields about one quart. But it is worth it.

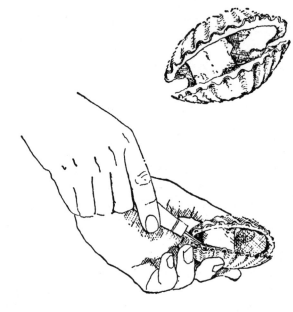

COOKING SCALLOPS

BROILED SCALLOPS

2 cups bay scallops
6 tablespoons melted butter
Juice from half lemon
½ teaspoon salt
¼ teaspoon pepper

Stir scallops in the melted butter until they are coated. Spread them out in a broiler. Broil for 10 minutes or until brown; sprinkle with the lemon juice and turn every few minutes so that they will brown evenly.

Serves 3–4.

SCALLOPS EN BROCHETTE

2 cups scallops
8 slices bacon
½ pound mushrooms

Wash and dry scallops. Cut bacon slices in thirds. Cut ends off mushrooms. Put a piece of bacon on the skewer first, a scallop next, then a mushroom cap. Continue this till skewer is filled. Brush with oil and broil over a white-coal fire until light brown. Or place on your broiling pan and broil, or, if you're lucky enough, broil in your electric broiler.

We like to do this outside while we enjoy the sunset.

SAUTÉED SCALLOPS

1 pint bay scallops
4 tablespoons butter
Toast points

I think that scallops have such a wonderful, delicate, elusive flavor of their own that they are best prepared in the simplest way.

Melt the butter in a pan and sauté the scallops until light golden. If they are truly fresh, a liquid will come from them. Pour the scallops and their juice over toast points. You might serve a lemon wedge.

Serves 3–4.

FRIED SCALLOPS

1 pint scallops
4 tablespoons bacon fat
½ cup flour

Roll scallops in flour. Heat fat about ½ inch deep in pan. Fry scallops until golden brown. Serve with tartare sauce and lemon. It only takes about 8 to 10 minutes.

Serves 3–4.

SCALLOPED SCALLOPS

1 pint bay scallops
1 cup cracker crumbs
1 cup top milk or medium cream
½ cup butter
½ teaspoon salt
⅛ teaspoon pepper
⅛ teaspoon nutmeg
1 cup bread crumbs

Put layer of cracker crumbs in a buttered casserole. Cover with the scallops; add half the cream; dot with butter; sprinkle with salt, pepper, and nutmeg. Add the bread crumbs and cover with the rest of the cream and butter. Bake at 350° for 30 minutes.

Serves 4 generously.

SOUTHAMPTON SCALLOPS

2 cups bay scallops
½ medium onion, minced, or 2 tablespoons chopped chives
2 tablespoons butter
1 10½-ounce can condensed cream of mushroom soup
2 tablespoons milk
1 teaspoon Worcestershire sauce
Dash cayenne pepper
¼ teaspoon salt
⅛ teaspoon pepper
½ cup grated Parmesan cheese

Sauté onion or chives gently in butter until yellow. Add the can of mushroom soup. Measure 2 tablespoons of milk and stir into the soup. Add the seasonings and scallops. Simmer softly for 10 minutes. Pack into individual baking shells. Sprinkle with Parmesan cheese. Brown under broiler.

Serves 4-6.

SCALLOPS WITH SAUCES

Scallops—at least ½ dozen per person
Open scallops and chill for several hours in the refrigerator.
Serve chilled with lemon juice

or

cocktail sauce

or

melted butter

This is the way the "natives" like them.

SCALLOPS WITH WINE

  1 pint scallops
  4 tablespoons butter
  ½ cup white wine (I like Chablis)
  2 tablespoons chopped fresh parsley
  Toast

Melt butter; add scallops, wine, and parsley. Sauté until golden and serve on toast.

Serves 3–4.

Towd Point Bouillabaisse

A friend needled me several summers to make some bouillabaisse. Now, I had enjoyed wonderful bouillabaisse in several fine French restaurants, but I never, never attempted to prepare any. Why? Well, whenever I came across a recipe it was too complicated in every way. I didn't have the time, ingredients, courage, or patience to go through with it.

However, the thought rankled in my mind. I hated to admit defeat. Suddenly one day the light dawned. The French were good cooks because they made the most of what they had on hand. I had on hand the greatest selection of seafood imaginable, so why not give it a try?

I came up with the following recipe which, I think, is one of my best. I would, however, like to suggest that you follow the French idea and use what you can obtain. For instance, we had Towd Point bouillabaisse the other night and I substituted soft-shell clams for hard clams, left out the crab meat, filleted large porgies and added more wine to stretch the dish, and it was better than ever. Take out some of the shells but leave some in for effect. If you're real cagey, you can leave them all in. If you're ravenous and serve nothing else for the meal, this will take care of two.

TOWD POINT BOUILLABAISSE

½ dozen cherrystone clams in shell
½ dozen oysters
½ cup crab meat
1 dozen mussels in shell (optional)
½ pound fillet of flounder
2 tablespoons butter
1 8-ounce can tomato sauce
½ cup water
½ teaspoon Italian seasoning or pinch of basil and bay leaf
Dash Worcestershire sauce
½ cup white wine (if desired)
¼ teaspoon salt
⅛ teaspoon pepper
½ teaspoon paprika

Scrub the shellfish. Cut the flounder in pieces and gently sauté it in the butter. Add everything else and simmer, covered, for 10 minutes. Serve with a slice of French bread on top and more on the side for dunking.

Serves 2–4.

SAVE SOME FOR NEXT SUMMER

Because some of our precious shellfish are disappearing, conservation rules have been adopted for their protection, and you should know about these.

Localities differ, I know, but the regulations of the Town of Southampton are fairly typical.

Hard clams must be one inch thick.

Soft clams or steamers must be two inches long.

Scallops (or escalops) must have one year's growth ring showing. No scallops can be taken from the water between January 1 and September 15.

Crabs must be five inches from point to point (of its shell), and no person shall catch any female crab bearing eggs. These look like sponge sacs hanging on the front of the crab.

Oysters may be taken only in months which have the letter "R" in them and must be three inches long.

So far as I know, there are no conservation rules in the East regarding mussels, but it is very important for you to know that mussels are quarantined along the entire coast of California from May until October. This is because they eat a plankton which is blooming during that time and which, assimilated by the mussels, causes them to poison humans.

Sauces for Shellfish

COCKTAIL SAUCE

1 12-ounce bottle chili sauce
Juice of ½ lemon
¼ cup horseradish
Dash Worcestershire sauce

Blend together. Will keep in refrigerator for quite a while. Use for clams on half shell, cold shrimp, crabs, and oysters on the half shell. It is even good spread on crackers!

It's fun to have this on hand when you come back from an afternoon's digging for clams. While you sort them and clean and open them, have this handy for sneaking some littlenecks.

HOT MELTED BUTTER

Good for dipping crabs, mussels, steamed clams, or oysters.
1 cup butter
2 teaspoons Worcestershire sauce
2 teaspoons prepared mustard
2 tablespoons chili sauce
2 drops Tabasco sauce
4 teaspoons lemon juice
2 teaspoons chopped parsley

Melt butter and add the rest of the seasonings. Heat until bubbly. Makes 1¾ cups.

George, the maître d' at the Beverly Hills Hotel in California, gave me this. He got it from *Sunset* magazine.

TARTARE SAUCE

- 1 cup mayonnaise
- 1 teaspoon finely minced onion
- 1 teaspoon finely minced pickle
- 1 tablespoon capers
- 1 tablespoon tarragon vinegar

Mix everything together and chill well. Makes about 1¼ cups.

GARLIC DIP

- 1 cup melted butter
- 2 crushed cloves garlic
- 1 teaspoon chopped parsley

Melt butter; add garlic and parsley and simmer for a few minutes.

Steamed cherrystones are delicious dunked in this.

VINEGAR SAUCE

(For Oysters)

- ½ cup vinegar
- ½ cup water
- ¼ teaspoon salt
- ⅛ teaspoon pepper
- Dash of Tabasco sauce

Mix vinegar, water, salt, pepper, and Tabasco sauce.

INDEX

L

Last-minute New England clam chowder, 27
Littleneck clams, 19
  on the half shell, 25
  Jean's appetizers, 24
  opening, 22
  and zucchini squash casserole, 36
Lobster broil, 61–62
Lobster with clam juice, Jan's, 66
Lobster crackers, 13
Lobster picks, 13
Lobster pots, 61
Lobster rolls, 65
  Vera's, 65
Lobsters, 59–68
  best eating, weight of, 61
  boiled, 63
  boiling, 62
  broiled, 63
  buying, 61
  charcoal-broiled, 64
  with clam juice, Jan's, 66
  cleaning, 61–62
  coral, 62
  Maine steamed, 64
  roe, 62
  rolls, 65
    Vera's, 65
  steaming, 62
  stuffings:
    clam, 67
    coral, 67

crab meat, 68
  plain, 67
  tomalley, 62
Lobster sauce, 66
Lobster shears, 13
Lobster stuffings, 67–68
  clam, 67
  coral, 67
  crab meat, 68
  plain, 67
Long Island, 11
Longneck clams. See Steamer clams

M

Maine steamed lobsters, 64
Maryland, crabbing in, 40–41
Maryland crab imperial, 48
Mecox Bay, 40
Melted butter, hot, 105
Montauk, L.I., 61
Motor Boating, 11
Mussel appetizer vinaigrette, 73
Mussels, 11, 69–77
  à la russe, 77
  appetizer vinaigrette, 73
  in bacon, 74
  beard of, 71
  Belgian, 74
  conservation rules, 101
  French, 75
  gathering, 71